# American indian being unique

AF176178

Peter Oberfrank – Hunziker

Impressum:

Bibliografische Information der Deutschen
Nationalbibliothek: Die Deutsche
Nationalbibliothek verzeichnet diese
Publikation in der Deutschen
Nationalbibliografie; detaillierte
bibliografische Daten sind im Internet über
www.dnb.de abrufbar.

Herstellung und Verlag:

BoD - Books on Demand, Norderstedt

ISBN 9783751956635

unique wedding

Big Love

This american indian being book is mainly in english language and also in german language and artfull and with good creativity doing forever.

Good NHL memories and good sport doing and celebrating …..

On 16 May every year I Peter Oberfrank – Hunziker celebrate forever with my NHL art name Kevin Lavallee my unique Kevin Lavallee day with NHL sports doing and good celebrating with laughing and enjoying good nature and just easy partying ….. also my NHL art names are Wayne Gretzky, Diego Maradona, Hansi Müller, Miami boy smiling, Peter New York Rangers, Montreal Canadiens Peter, family Peter, sporty Peter, happy Peter, nature Peter,

party Peter, Peter hearty, Merek
Doughy, NHLing Peter, Martin St.
Louis, Pezi, Los Angeles Peter …..
NHL sport is happy doing and being
with pleasure and for me with good
memories and unique being and in heart
being and orange being …..

deep blue heart house with sporty place
and nature place ….. forever true being
and family being and happy smiling

„Good morning family"

„Happy sports doing"

„Enjoying"

„smiling"

„green house being"

„unique celebrating"

„working"

„spacing"
Aborigines house
wood    stones    waterfalls
woodywoodpeckerhouse    stonyhouse
wateringhouse
brown house with white church and
sports fields and garden and happy
being disco in marmor style and NHL
museum

ET flower power house
„good dancing with the mouse"

Mickey mouse house
basketball area and flowers garden

Rapperswil sports stadium
New York Madison Square Garden
Chicago Blackhawks waterfalls house
Las Vegas Golden Knights sporty and
nature house
Los Angeles circling house

deep blue heart being

Peter Oberfrank, geboren am 27. November 1971 in Rapperswil Zürich, Schweiz Amerika, und mit meinem Ehenamen Peter Oberfrank - Hunziker ewig glücklich verheiratet mit Michelle Hunziker und viele glückliche Kinder in der Familie. Neben dem NHL Sport und der beruflichen Arbeit als Techniker und Naturarbeiter bereitet mir auch das Schreiben und Lesen von Büchern sowie das Zeichnen und Malen große Freude und ein Museum besuchen und auch einfach in der Natur sein und Party machen und lachen und grinsen.

Bienen house in Boston

Good and funny living in Boston Bruins house micky with wicky being and lanaön being and grinselen …..

butterflies seeing and dancing

Chicago flori house being and good partylen dancing and 100 goals in football goal scoring

ET flotschi paryting

New York Rangers fully happy flowering housing and singing and sportyling in New York Central park region

Hall of NHL museum

NHL museumhouse forever

Region Germany woodstonehouse

NHL all stars marmorgolding housing with beaching in New York

American Indian sporting area and cosy housing colourful with remembering

and books and flower partying and
being in Madison Square Garden
Trainings Center

Luen city living and partying

Yeahi living

Lago di Garda in Lazise in America
Miami living with big rounding sey and
palm beaches

Big sea beaches with colourful trees in
River plate sporty stadium for football
playing and living in woodpalms houses
in Argentina

Gardaseeyo and Gardasee being in
Italien with bluewhite jerseying being
and Pipo dancingstyle

Also funny NHL art names for me Peter
Oberfrank – Hunziker are Pipo,
Gorosito, Zenga, Vialli, Donadoni,

Pezzey, Joe Thornton, Pertl, Party dancing, Nashvilli, Clowni …..

Amazonas Delta living in funky and hippie houses and grinsying

Arizona dschungel living

Rapperswil church living and moon and stars looking

Tampa Bay castle house living

NHL homing

Nashville Leopards house living with waterfalling and raining partys and Life is a journey and in Rapperswil „Kirschblütenfest" good celebrating

Rose garden living in Sao Paolo in Brasil and in Maracana football stadium beautiful soccer selecao playing and on mountain Zuckerhut with lemonhut living

On oasis dschungo way travelling to Argentina football stadium and good and arty and creative football playing and just Nike sportsdresses enjoying

In Atzteka Mexiko sportfootall stadium ever World team cup trophy celebrating soccerlo and easy and cheasy being

Dieses indianische einzigartige Buch ist ein „Große Liebe Heiratsversprechen" von mir Peter Oberfrank – Hunziker an meine Ehefrau Michelle mit schöner Tiefe und glücklich sein im Herzen und ewiges Erinnern an unsere roten Herzpolster und grünen Herzpolster mit ewiger Treue und fröhliches Feiern beim Weihnachtsbaum mit Geschenken und Ostern feiern in der Natur und schön wohnen und reisen und am Geburtsort freudig sein und spaßig NHL Sport machen und Trophäen feiern und Confetti basteln und schöne Bilder malen und Bücher lesen und auch Bücher schreiben und im Weltall sein und überall sein und ewig schöne Graswiesen genießen und am Wassersteg witzig sein und schöne Modekleidung tragen und wunderbare Essensfeiern und Party machen und in Kirchen die Atmospähre schätzen und Sternbilder schauen und schöne Wasserfälle anschauen und Ruhe genießen und Palmenbäume bestaunen und in schönen Sportstadien sein und genau sein und clownig sein …..


An einem Sonnentag ist ein schöner Festivaltag zum Feiern und schön sein mit NHL Sport und die Natur ewig genießen und im „History book" ist dieser Tag als „Indianertag" bezeichnet und mit „glücklich sein" beschrieben …..

Dieses Buch ist auch schön zum Erinnern und einer meiner NHL art names ist „happy" für glücklich sein und diesen NHL art name habe ich nur bei den NHL Mannschaften New York Rangers und Nashville Predators und Fußballteam Argentina mit der Rückennumer „24" und meinem „Heiratsname Peter Oberfrank – Hunziker" und NHL art name „happy" am Jersey getragen und dies immer und ewig. Meinen Geburtsnamen „Peter Oberfrank" und Rückennumer „27" und „happy celebrating" habe ich bei allen NHL Mannschaften am Jersey getragen und dies auch immer und ewig …. dies steht auch im NHL Trophy book so geschrieben …. für mich glückliche NHL art names sind auch Sbornaja, Czech, Yvgeni Malkin, Wayne Gretzky,

Martin St. Louis, nature, all star, mascoti, toronti, Peter ever, red, green, orange, newyorky.

Die NHL ist freudiger Sport und auch schöne Kinderfeste.

Ein Rosenfest und Zirkuszeltfest bei meinem Geburtsort Rapperswil am Zürichsee in der Schweiz und ein großes NHL New York Fest im Madison Square Garden.

NHL Museumfest in Washington und Buchfest in Oklahoma und Palmenfest in Dallas.

Herzfest in Chicago und Naturfest in Homburg und Theaterfest in Köln und Philosophiefest im ET Land und ganz fröhliches Sportmodenfest in San Francisco.

Hawai festival and orando festivaling

unique festivaling orangeyellow and
yeahi being

Wasserfest in Hamburg

Waldfest in Buffalo und Schiffefest in
Columbus und Moosfest in Philadelphia

Naturglanzfest in ewigi und Steinefest
in Region Germany

indiany hearty

Los Angeles being and NHL sporting
forever and celebrating and wedding
and family being and nice being and
indiany being and musicing and dancing
and white hearting and remembering
red polstering and memoring and joying
and NHL icehockey playing and
footballing and being with pleasure and
unique celebrating …..

NHL icehockeyplaying in Chicago and
doing sports and nice visits from
Barbara Fiegl with Kristiane Backer
fashion clothing and sporty visits from
Berry and sporting visits from Günther
and happy visits from Aborigines and
joyful visits from ET and
flowergardening and Huzi festivaly and
colourful visits from Cologno girly and
sportive visits from Boston boys and
CSKA boys and referees and fans ….

Blumenfest in St. Louis und
Architekturtechnikfest in Detroit und
Kunstausstellungsfest in Los Angeles
und Vulkanfest in Calgary und
Sandwüstenfest in Winnipeg mit
Wiesenglitzer und Palmwüstenfest in
Afrika und Wörtherseefest in
Klagenfurt und Musikfest in Dallas ….

Strandfest am Meer in Vancouver und
Bärenfest mit See schauen in Minnesota
und Fußballfest in München und
Basketballfest in Orunda und Wüstefest
in der Sahara und Dschungelfest in
Bulongo und Blumifest in Australien
und Sternzungofestival.

Zeichenmalfest in asian

# Höhlenfest in Homburg und Bastelfest in Hamburg

## Hochzeitsmodefest in Zürich

Palmenfest in Palm Springs

Miami boy smiling fest in Miami city
for me Peter Oberfrank – Hunziker and
family being and white festival

yellow Oberfrank familying

orange Hunziker familyo

red Valentinitsch redo

blue Vonn smilinge

grünp Fiegl nicingly

NHLY

Eisfest in Hawai


Schifest in motunga mountain und
Partylingfest in lakoi in Vail indianic
region with silver trophy and gold
trophy and happy dancing …..


NHL glory festival with sporting and
musicing and dancing and happyling in
miamying and housing and celebrating
NHL sportivo trophy skyblue


Eskimofest in Polari


South african festo in indianicy region
southpoling and southypolarig

Indianerzeltfest in Südpolari

Parkfest in New York und Moosfest in siloi

Fichtenbaumfest in Arizona und
Tannenbaumfest in Las Vegas



spacy being and spaciyo
Space shuttle celebrating and
remembering heartyly meadows

Sombrerohutfest in Mexiko

Schneefest in Salt Lake City


NHL museums festivals with
chicagostylingcska dancing with
Yonsho and Oleg Tichonow and Allain
Vigneaut and Jeff Gorton and happyling
and ET dancing and in Swiss Almöhi
festy and Heidi blumoso festu and
Claudine seerosen festivalo and sports
stadium Zürichsee festovalongo and
calm areas festivals and intellect parties
and funny being and Cologno girl
fashion styling parties and sport parties
worldwide and Hippie parties

Vier Jahreszeitenfest in Florida und
Föhrenfest in Montreal

Zwetschgenfest und Marillenfest und Apfelfest und Birnenfest und Kartoffelfest und Maracujafest und Zitronenfest und Kokosnussfest und Orangenfest in Ottawa

Farbenfest in Minnesota und Tierefest
und Pfanzenfest in Nashville

Wasserglanzfest in St. Louis …..
NHL trophy St. Louis year 2004
celebrating and roundballo dancing
festival forever and sporting

Forever young     rosawhite church
naming and cherrishing church in
Miami with written papers with names
originally Peter Oberfrank – Hunziker
with funny forever NHL art names like
Wayne Gretzky, Christian Perthaler,
Martin St. Louis, Marc Messier, Mario
Lemieux, Lundqvist, indiany and
Michelle Hunziker with our children
Aurora and Michaela and Leila and
Anna and Elke Valentinitsch with our
Children Miri and Tiri and Liri and
Amelie and Linea and Lindsey Vonn
with our child Alice and Isabel Tüchtler
with our children Elisabeth and Isabelo
and Elisbetha and Michelor and
Michelar family being and Barbara
Fiegl with childs Kristiano and
Kristiana and nice being and NHLy

creative doing

NHL ist auch mit indianigen Zeichen
wie \*\*\* und /;;)= und :-:

Kirchenfeste überall

yeah New York NHL sport parc festival with glorying in silver in ewigi and in america with gloryo in golden in central park and Madison Square garden sports stadium and Cologno sports stadium with laughing and partying

Tanzmusikfest in Köln und Opernfest in Calgary und Strandlauffest in Tampa Bay und Ruhefest in Ruondo

Heiratstempelfest in Dehli ….. mit
Farben wie weiß und grün und blau und
rot und gelb …..

All star Fest in New York yankeei
stadium und lustiges sportliches
Mascoti icefestival in Miami und NFL
festi in Miami mit NHL medali mascoti

Grasglitzerbaumfest in Chiri …..

NHL Weihnachtsosterfest überall ....

Modefest und Sandfest und Baumfest
und Grasfest und Wasserfest und
Wetterfest und Blumenfest und
Sonnefest und Nachtfest

ewig Heiratsfest und glücklich lachen
und fröhlich sein und witzelen in Zürich
und Enjoy Fest in Asian und nature
festival in Indianiyo und woodi festi in
wolundo

lachen

glücklich sein
happy being

Hundertwasserhaus colourig living in
New York dancing area and being in
New York Yankees stadium celebrating

NYR Statue of Liberty living and american indians tents in New York Island living and goofy skiing

Rome journeying in Italy to Neapel and Sicilia and Troumadour and Chisa and Bergamo and Milano and Torino and Bern and Chusla and asian city and Homburg citystyling and Köln citylorelei and Barcelona spainy football stadium and to gran area sportyfootball Nashville stadiums with NHL shops and NHL museums area and people meeting and nature meeting places and living in fairy tale castleungo

Vancouver fashionstyling house

Ottawa dancing house and yoga area

Minnesota village housing with children area and pleasure place

Los Angeles dancing area with Huzi
being and smiling and gardening …..
tenty living

Los Angeles villas living homing and celebrating NHL trophies and funny being

Luen cathedral living

Detroit dancing hall with high
creativeness living indianisch and
clownisch ….. colourful marmorig
stone with rounding and threeecking
and glimpsing and ruhing and eloying
…..


happy funny bunny dancing

Boston Bruins music hall and joyfull
celebrating

Montreal Canadiens beaching house


Toronto staring house and joyo dancing
and woody living

Linzisch plateaus living and
woodstyliongo and discoling and
castele living


London bus driving and happilen

Pyramides in Egypt living

Tento plateau houses marmory and
woddyzo styling being and Africa
enjoying and skiilen

Detroito africayo sportstadium with big
partying

South pole easy homeleno

Äquator good creato living

North pole cooly living

Hawai living good enjoying
marmorcolourig and beachongyo

San Francisco styling living


San Francisco Road and Bridge to
Tokyo and China


Nature ways blue and red


Los Angeles NHL celebrating with
orange fashion clothing and in heart
being unique and smiling


colourful ways

Calgary fashionable living style and pleasuring

Snowi house

Australian Melbourne house with big palms and monkeys and elefants and many pets and plants ….......

San Diego sport by Nashville area with houese villaging on sea beach and creative and integrative sports doing and enjoying

Chicago disco doming with coople roof and castle towers and main housing and funny disco with sporting and hoopylingo dancing and hoopsyluyo dancing and hoopsyrungo dancing and witzelen and nice eating and nice drinking in restaurant and talking on balcoon and remembering and doing sport and celebrating and joyingfullindiany…..

grey festival
ET tongo dancing and playing football
again with the football Tango and tongo
dschungel area living

cyan festival
good celebrating

Rapperswil castle house living and joyfullo fairy tales

Anaheim beach villas living and
journeying to St. Lousi for good skiing

Los Angeles hills living houses with
great sea looks and relaxing and joyful
being on the beach


flower colourig gardening

Region Germany sporty being

Köln sport arena and fashion shows and dancing sessions

Hungary sport styling

Long time in Miami region with beach
joying

Gösser City Innsbruck being with
tentoindiany sport making and dancing
and celebrating NHL trophies and
Vulcano celebrating and Vulcan
museum partying and NHL sport doing
and NHL trophies celebrating and good
partying on orientalic grande partyo and
funny dancing and happilen and
homingyo and memories and funny
doing …..

being creative

green land country being and seeing
water areas

palm land being and colours enjoying

funny figl skiing in Calgary and playing
icehockey in Calgary Flames NHL
sportivo stadium with many fans …..

wandering around

architectual thinking and doing

NHL all stars celebrating

NHL trophies in NHL museums
celebrating


good enjoying

happy being

true is good

unique being

running and Yoga sport doing

watching funny television shows

sporty doing

For me Peter Oberfrank – Hunziker are also good NHL art names Peter Gösser, Peter Coca Cola, Peter Nike, Peter MTV Coca Cola report, Peter NHL forever, Peter housing, Peter celebrating, Peter partying, Peter mountaining, Peter ÖBB Buffalo, Peter technic Boston, Yaromir Yagr, Thomas Vanek, Leon Draisaitl, Peter Macnamara, Yurov, Surov, Gallander, Nash, Tretjak, Richter, Krutow, Yagrov, tento, Holst, Murray, Stankiewicz, homingyo, Zürichseefestival, winterwonderland, chicagoyi, edmonty, Hippie …..

funny mountainbike touring on small
mountains with beautiful and unique
bachwater and wonderful trees and
green and fine weather with sunshine
and clouds in luen indiany land


joyfull gaming
NHL Chicagoyi trophy happy
celebrating forever and remembering
heart memories and indiany dancing
and dreaming and being and playing
NHL forever and forever young and
joyi


rosa Rosen Buch

nature enjoying and NHL sport doing
and partying and celebrating


orange NHL


forever celebrating